CONTENTS

This collection contains all the songs written
by Led Zeppelin from their first 5 albums.

©1973 SUPERHYPE PUBLISHING
All Rights Reserved

LED ZEPPELIN I

HOW MANY MORE TIMES

Words and Music by
JIMMY PAGE, JOHN PAUL JONES
and JOHN BONHAM

Moderately fast

EXTRA WORDS (spoken)

I was a young man, I couldn't resist
Started thinkin' it over, just what I had missed.
Got me a girl and I kissed her and then and then
Whoops, oh Lordy, well I did it again.
Now I got ten children of my own
I got another child on the way, that makes eleven.
But you know, I'm in constant heaven
I know it's all right in my mind
I got a little schoolgirl and she's all mine
I can't get through to her 'cause it doesn't permit
But I'm gonna give her everything I've got to give.

Oh, Rosie, oh, girl
Oh, Rosie, oh, girl
Steal away now, steal away
Steal away baby, steal away
Little Robert Anthony wants to come and play.

Why don't you come to me baby?
Steal away, all right, all right...

They call me the hunter, that's my name
They call me the hunter, that's how I got my fame
Ain't no need to hide,
Ain't need to run
'Cause I've got you in the sights of my .... gun!

How many more times barrelhouse all night long?
How many more times barrelhouse all night long?
I've got to get to you, baby
Baby, please come home.
Why don't you please come home?
Why don't you please come home?

▶ Special note to guitarists from **JIMMY PAGE:**

Try the rhythm chords in the 5th position:

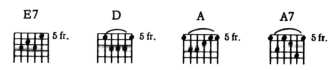

E7   D   A   A7

BABE, I'M GONNA LEAVE YOU

Words and Music by
ANNE BREDON, JIMMY PAGE
and ROBERT PLANT

Repeat and fade

ADDITIONAL WORDS

I know, I know, I know, I never, I never, I never, I never, I never leave you, baby
But I got to go away from this place, I've got to quit you.
Ooh, baby, baby, baby, baby
Baby, baby, baby, ooh don't you hear it callin'?
Woman, woman, I know, I know it's good to have you back again
And I know that one day baby, it's really gonna grow, yes it is.
We gonna go walkin' through the park every day.
Hear what I say, every day.
Baby, it's really growin', you made me happy when skies were grey.
But now I've got to go away
Baby, baby, baby, baby
That's when it's callin' me
That's when it's callin' me back home ...

► Note to guitarists from **JIMMY PAGE:**

The basic chords in the progression to this song should be varied by using extensions.

The "Spanish bit" as Jimmy calls it (see ① on the arrangement) is played as follows:

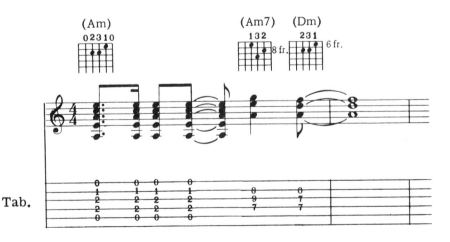

COMMUNICATION BREAKDOWN

Words and Music by
JIMMY PAGE, JOHN PAUL JONES
and JOHN BONHAM

Moderate Rock

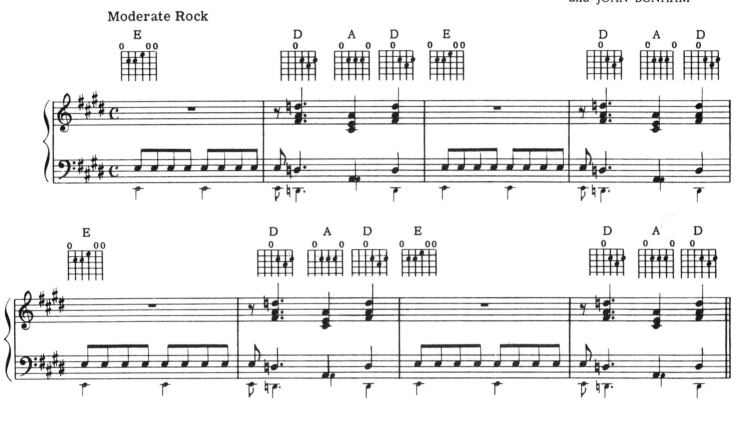

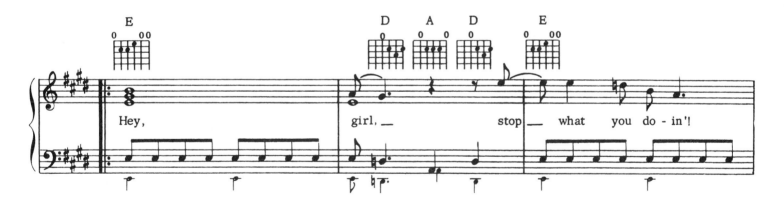

Hey, girl, __ stop __ what you do-in'!

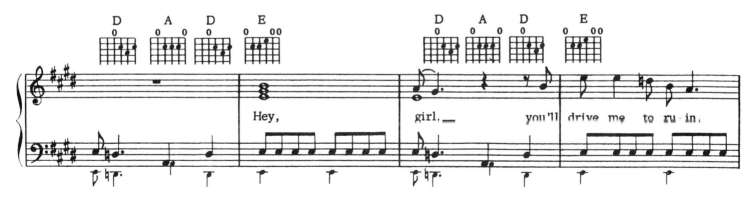

Hey, girl, __ you'll drive me to ru-in.

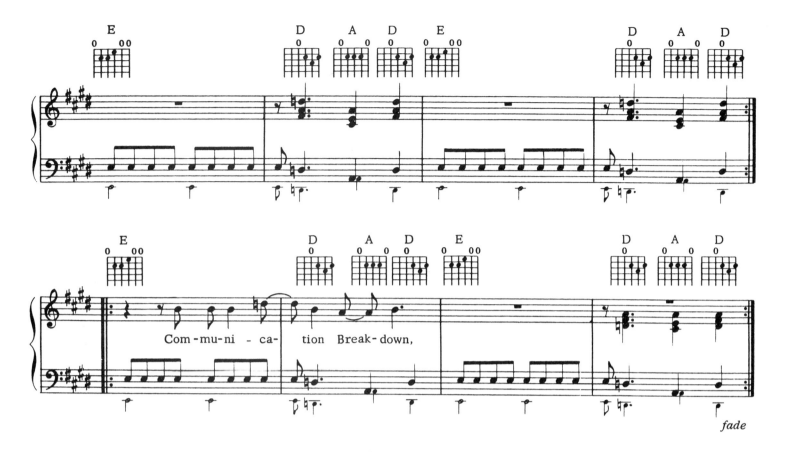

Com-mu-ni - ca- tion Break-down,

fade

ADDITIONAL WORDS

Hey! Girl, I got something I think you ought to know
Hey! Babe, I wanna tell you that I love you so
I wanna hold you in my arms, yeah!
I'm never gonna let you go,
Yes, I like your charms.

Chorus

▶ **Note to guitarists from JIMMY PAGE:**

The basic background figure of this tune can best be played in the V position.

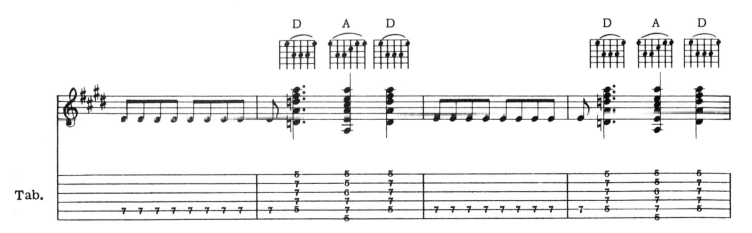

Tab.

GOOD TIMES BAD TIMES

Words and Music by
JIMMY PAGE, JOHN PAUL JONES
JOHN BONHAM and ROBERT PLANT

at home. I don't care what the neighbors say,

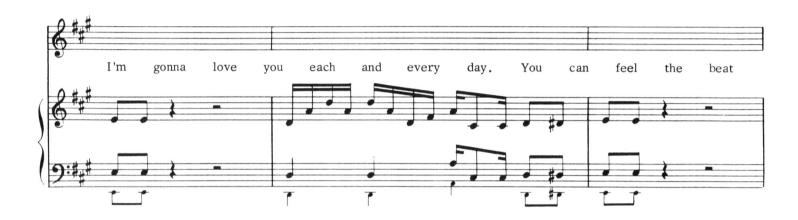

I'm gonna love you each and every day. You can feel the beat

within my heart. Realize, sweet babe, we ain't ever gonna part.

fade

▶ **Note to guitarists from JIMMY PAGE:**

I play the repeated figure in the first part of the song like this:

etc.

Tab.

DAZED AND CONFUSED

Words and Music by
JIMMY PAGE

Slow Blues

(No chords, bass line only)

1. Been dazed and con-fused ____ for so long it's not true,

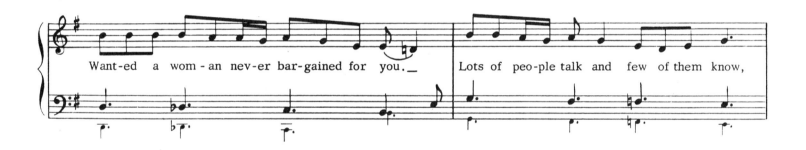

Want-ed a wom-an nev-er bar-gained for you.__ Lots of peo-ple talk and few of them know,

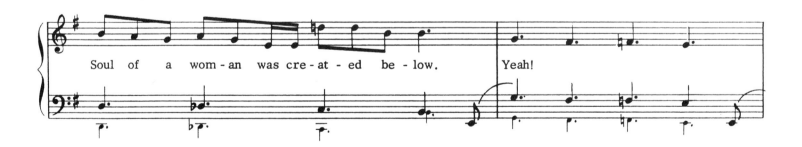

Soul of a wom-an was cre-at-ed be-low. Yeah!

2. You

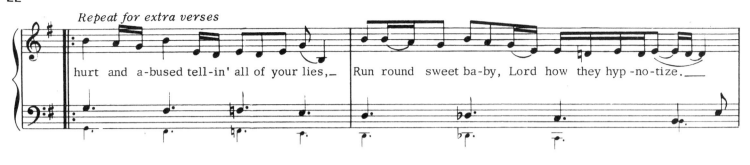

Repeat for extra verses

hurt and a-bused tell-in' all of your lies,_ Run round sweet ba-by, Lord how they hyp-no-tize.___

Sweet lit-tle ba-by, I don't know where you've been,_ Oh, I love you ba-by, here I come a-gain._

②   *last time to Coda* ⊕

3.(Ev-'ry)

Coda ⊕

Repeat and fade

Verse

3. Every day, I work so hard
   Bringin' home my hard earned pay
   Try to love you baby, but you push me away.
   Don't know where you're goin'
   I don't know just where you've been,
   Sweet little baby, I want you again.

4. Been dazed and confused for so long,
   It's not true
   Wanted a woman never bargain for you.
   Take it easy baby, let them say what they will
   Will your tongue wag so much when I send you the bill.

Notes from LED ZEPPELIN

Jimmy: Here's how to play the bass figure at ①

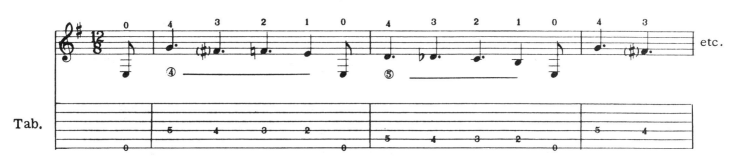

John: Here's the same figure on bass

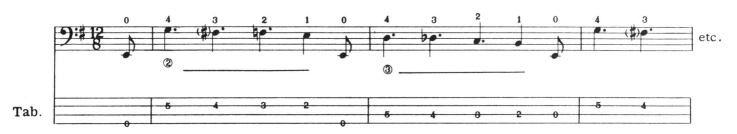

Jimmy: Here's the break at ②

BLACK MOUNTAIN SIDE

Words and Music by
JIMMY PAGE

Special note from Jimmy Page: I use a special tuning on this modal melody. Tune the 1st string down one full tone to D; tune the 2nd string down one full tone to A; leave the 3rd, 4th and 5th strings as is; tune the 6th string down one full tone to D. I use a flat pick to bring out the bass line and play the upper notes with the middle and ring fingers. The following arrangement contains the main theme in traditional and tablature notation.

YOUR TIME IS GONNA COME

Words and Music by
JIMMY PAGE and JOHN PAUL JONES

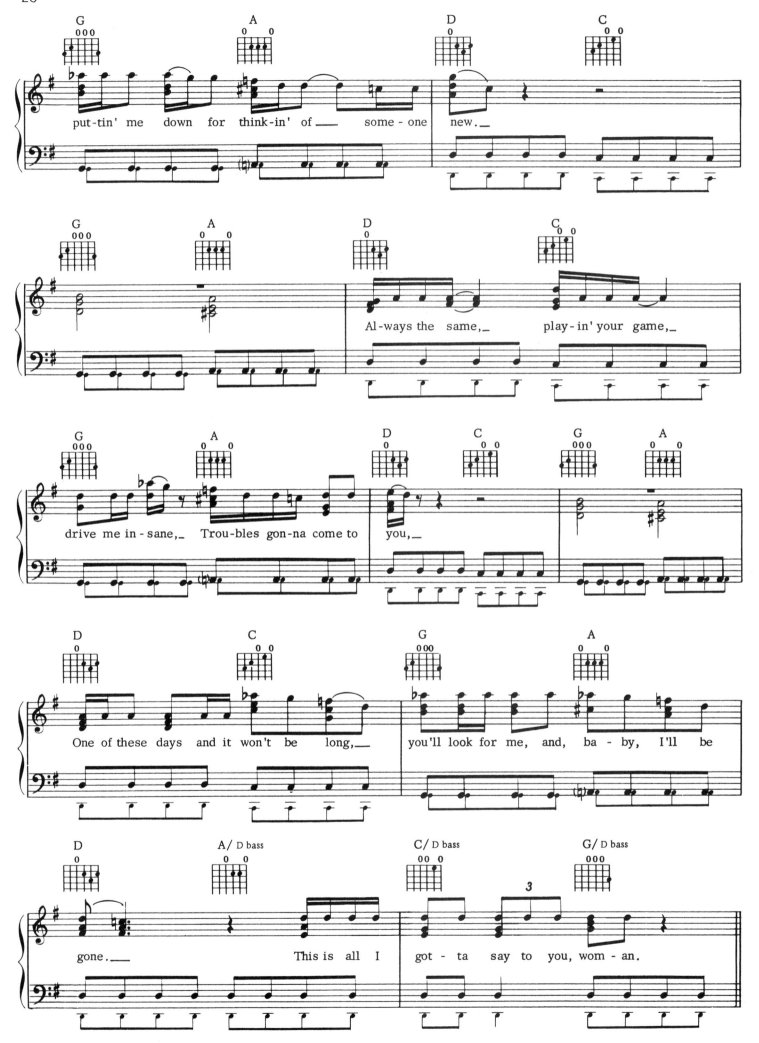

Verse

2. Made up my mind to break you this time,
Won't be so fine, it's my turn to cry.
Do what you want, I won't take the brunt.
It's fadin' away, can't feel you anymore
Don't care what you say 'cause I'm gone away to stay,
Gonna make you pay for the great big hole in my heart.
People talkin' all around,
Watch out woman, no longer is
The joke gonna be in my heart.
You been bad to me woman,
But it's comin' back home to you.

Chorus

LED ZEPPELIN II

WHOLE LOTTA LOVE

Words and Music by
JIMMY PAGE, ROBERT PLANT,
JOHN PAUL JONES and JOHN BONHAM

Chorus

Wan-na Whole Lot-ta Love?___   Wan-na Whole Lot-ta Love?_

(Last time D. S. and fade with bass figure) 𝄋

Wan-na Whole Lot-ta Love?___   You've been

(Last time D. S. and fade with bass figure)

Additional Words

You've been learnin'
Baby, I mean learnin'
All them good times, baby, baby
I've been yearnin'
Way, way down inside
Honey, you need it
I'm gonna give you my love,
I'm gonna give you my love.
     Chorus

You've been coolin'
Baby, I've been droolin'
All the good times
I've been misusin'
Way, way down inside
I'm gonna give you my love,
I'm gonna give you every inch of my love,
Gonna give you my love.
     Chorus

Way down inside, woman,
You need love.

(Spoken:)
Shake for me, girl
I wanna be your backdoor man.
Hey, oh, hey, oh
Oh, oh, oh
Keep a-coolin', baby,
Keep a-coolin', baby.
     (fade)

RAMBLE ON

Words and Music by
JIMMY PAGE and ROBERT PLANT

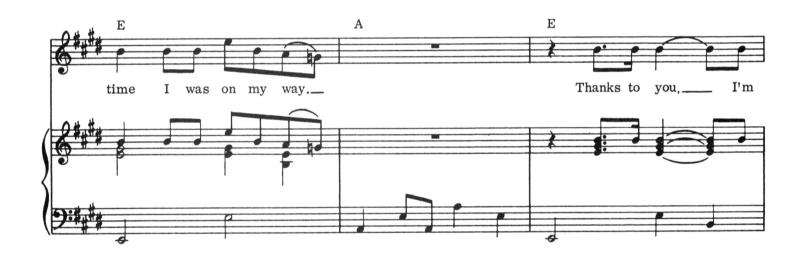

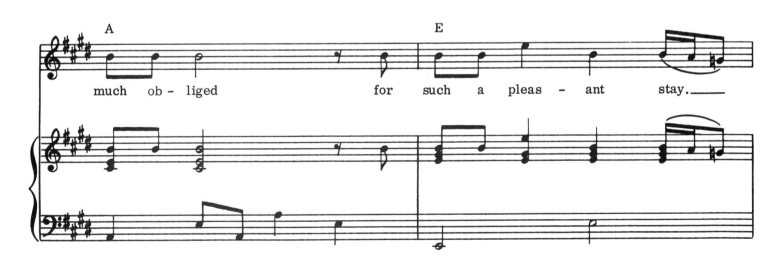

Chorus

Been this way ten years to the day,_ Ram-ble On,_ Find the queen of all my dreams,

Got no time to spend and weep, The time has come to be gone._ And

tho' our health we drank a thou-sand times, Have to Ram-ble On.

D. C. till fade

Additional Words

2. Mine's a tale that can't be told,
   My freedom I hold dear;
   How many years ago in days of old
   When magic filled the air
   T'was in the darkest depths of Mordor
   I met a girl so fair
   But golem, the evil one crept up
   And slipped away with her.
   Her, her . . . . yea
   Ain't nothing I can do.
   (Chorus and fade)

MOBY DICK

Music by
JOHN BONHAM, JOHN PAUL JONES
and JIMMY PAGE

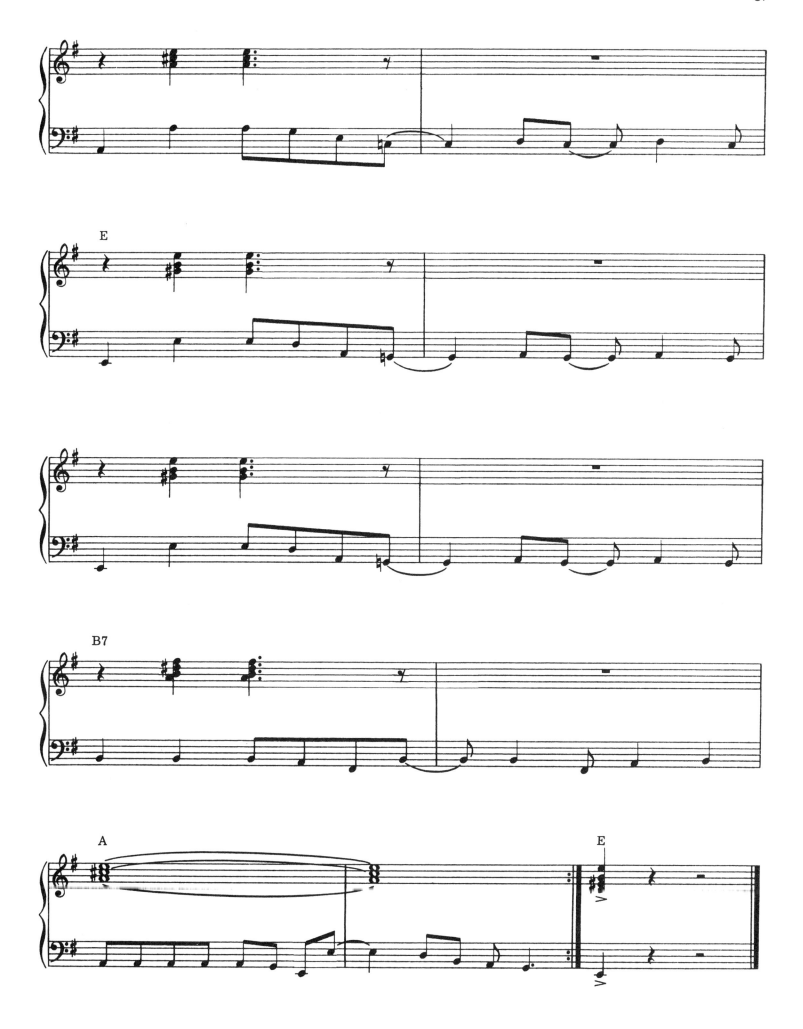

HEARTBREAKER

Words and Music by
JIMMY PAGE, ROBERT PLANT,
JOHN PAUL JONES and JOHN BONHAM

Slow Blues

1. Hey fel-las, have you heard the news?_ You know that An-nie's back in town.__ It

won't take long, just watch and see an' the fel-las lay their mon-ey down.__ Her

style is new but the face is the same as it was so long a-go,__ But

from her eyes__ is a dif-f'rent smile like that

Fine (1st time) *D. C.*

of one who knows.__

(Tacet chords)

Peo - ple talk - in' all a - round 'bout the way you left me flat,

I don't care what the peo - ple say, I know where their jive is at.

One thing I do have on my mind, if you can clar - i - fy please do,___ It's the

D. S. al Fine 𝄋

way you call me by an-oth-er guy's name when I try to make love___ to you!___ 𝄋

D. S. al Fine

Additional Words

2. Well, it's been ten years and maybe more
   Since I first set eyes on you;
   The best years of my life gone by,
   Here I am alone and blue.
   Some people cry and some people die
   By the wicked ways of love;
   But I'll just keep on rollin' along
   With the grace of the Lord above.

3. Work so hard I couldn't unwind,
   Get some money saved;
   Abuse my love a thousand times,
   However hard I tried.
   Heartbreaker, your time has come,
   Can't take your evil ways;
   Go away,
   Heartbreaker.

THANK YOU

Words and Music by
JIMMY PAGE and ROBERT PLANT

Additional Words

And so today, my world it smiles
Your hand in mine we walk the miles
Thanks to you it will be done
For you to me are the only one
Happiness no more be sad
Happiness . . . . I'm glad

WHAT IS AND WHAT SHOULD NEVER BE

Words and Music by
JIMMY PAGE and ROBERT PLANT

Slow Blues

And if I say to you to-mor-row,

Take my hand, child, come with me.

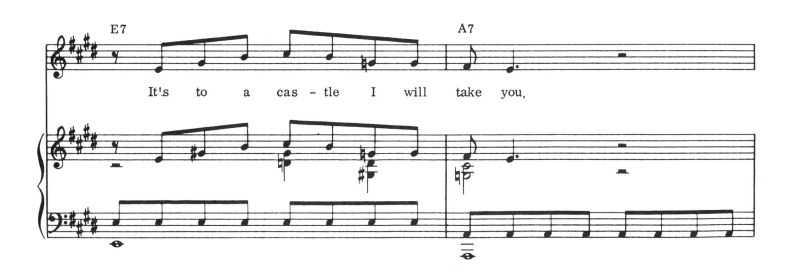

It's to a cas-tle I will take you,

tak - in' our time.___ Ooh!_____

(2. And if you say to me to)

Additional Words

2. And if you say to me tomorrow
   Oh what fun it all would be
   Then what's to stop us, pretty baby
   But what is and what should never be.
   (Repeat Chorus)

3. So if you wake up with the sunrise
   And all your dreams are still as new
   And happiness is what you need so bad
   Girl, the answer lies with you, yeah.
   (Repeat Chorus)

LIVING LOVING MAID
(She's Just A Woman)

Words and Music by
JIMMY PAGE and ROBERT PLANT

Chorus

Come on, babe__ on the round-a-bout,__ ride on the mer-ry-go-round,__ We all know__ what your name__ is, so you bet-ter lay your mon-ey down._____

Liv - in', lov - in', she's just a wom - an.

Liv - in', lov - in', she's just a wom - an.

Additional Words

2. Alimony, alimony payin' your bills,
   Livin', lovin', she's just a woman
   When your conscience hits you, knock it back with pills.
   Livin', lovin', she's just a woman.
   (Chorus)

3. Tellin' tall tales of how it used to be.
   Livin', lovin', she's just a woman.
   With the butler and the maid and the servants three.
   Livin', lovin', she's just a woman.
   (Chorus)

4. Nobody hears a single word you say.
   Livin', lovin', she's just a woman.
   But you keep on talkin' till your dyin' day.
   Livin', lovin', she's just a woman.
   (Chorus)

LED ZEPPELIN III

IMMIGRANT SONG

Words and Music by
JIMMY PAGE and ROBERT PLANT

Ah, _____ ah, _____

We come from the land of the ice and snow, from the

mid-nite sun where the hot springs blow, ___ the ham-mer of the gods will

Since I've Been Loving You

Words and Music by
JIMMY PAGE, ROBERT PLANT
and JOHN PAUL JONES

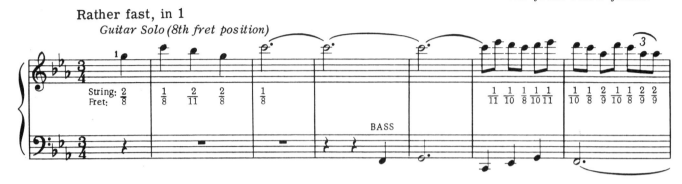

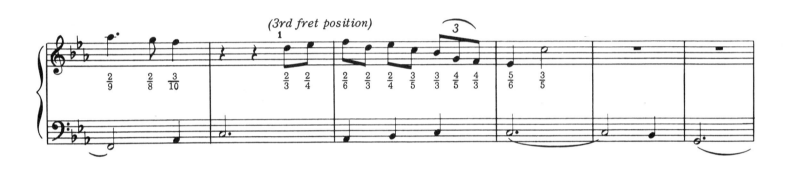

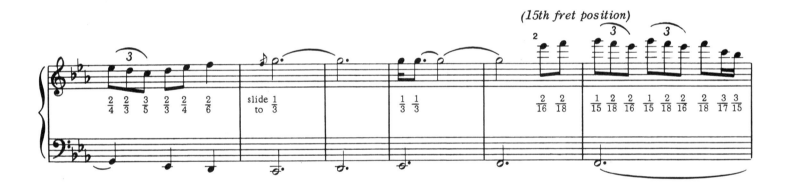

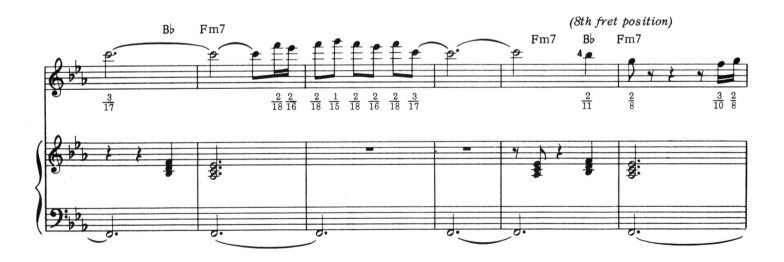

Since — I've Been Lov-ing You,

I'm a-bout to lose _____ my wor-ried mind.

(Piano continues chordal accompaniment)

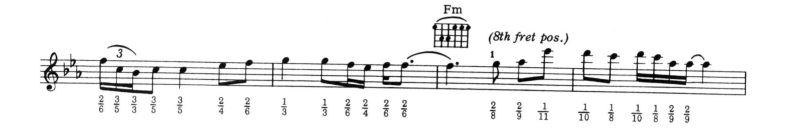

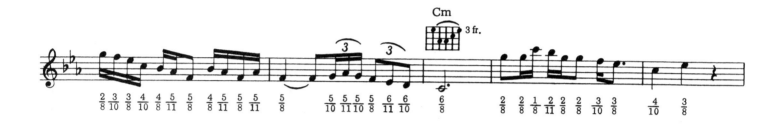

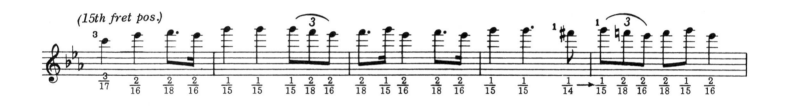

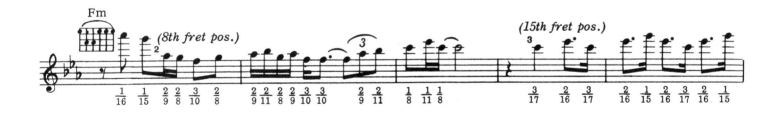

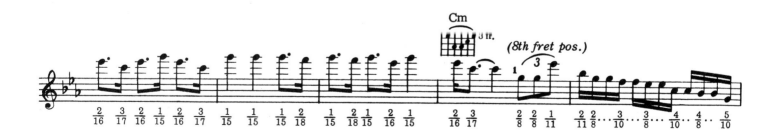

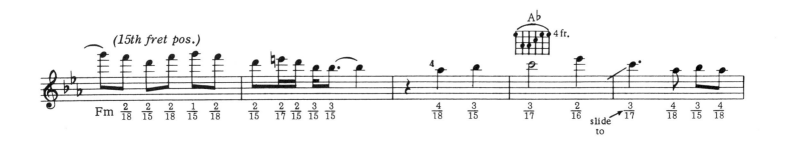

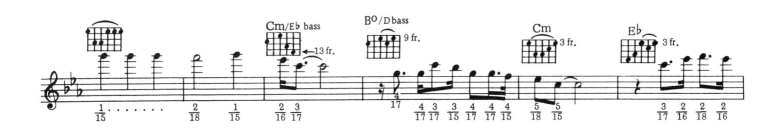

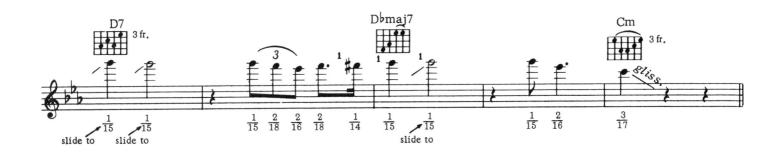

TANGERINE

Words and Music by
JIMMY PAGE

GALLOWS POLE

Traditional Arrangement by
JIMMY PAGE and ROBERT PLANT

Hang-man, __ hang-man, __ hold it a lit-tle while, think I see my friends com-ing, rid-ing man-y a mile. __

Friends, did you get some

78

OUT ON THE TILES

Words and Music by
JIMMY PAGE, ROBERT PLANT
and JOHN BONHAM

82

Oooh yeah, ooh yeah, _____

ooh yeah, oh yeah. _____ I'm so glad I'm liv-ing and gon-na

tell the world I am, I got me a fine wo-man and she

says that I'm her man, _ one thing that I know for sure _ gon-na

THAT'S THE WAY

Words and Music by
JIMMY PAGE and ROBERT PLANT

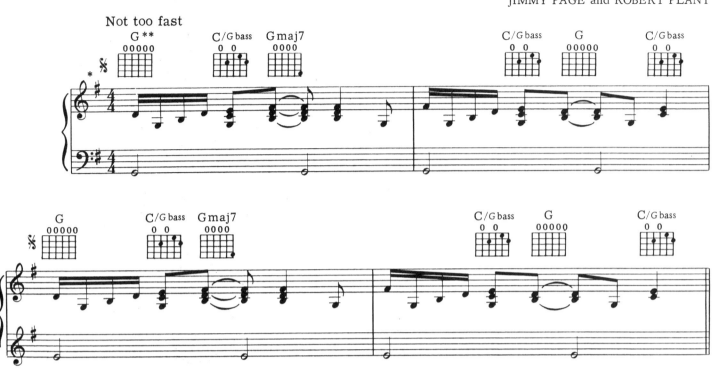

I don't know how I'm gon-na tell you
And yes-ter-day I saw you standing by the river,

I can't play with you no
and weren't those tears that filled your

more,
eyes,

I don't know how I'm gon-na do what ma-ma told me,
And all the fish that lay in dir-ty wa-ter dy-ing,

* Recorded ½ step lower (Gb Major)

** Guitarists use G tuning: 6th string = D   5th string = G   4th string = D
3rd string = G   2nd string = B   1st string = D

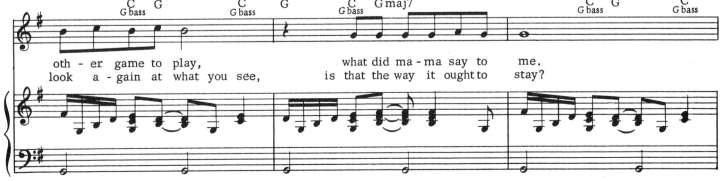

And when I'm out I see you walk — ing —
I don't know what to say a - bout it,

why don't your eyes see me,
when all your ears have turned a - way,

could it be you've found an -
but now's the time to look and

oth - er game to play,
look a - gain at what you see,

what did ma - ma say to me.
is that the way it ought to stay?

BRON-Y-AUR STOMP

Words and Music by
JIMMY PAGE, ROBERT PLANT
and JOHN PAUL JONES

Rhythm
* Guitarists: Capo up 3 frets. Guitar in D tuning: 6th string = D,   5th string = A,   4th string = D,
3rd string = F#,   2nd string = A,   1st string = D

coun-try lane, I'll be sing-ing a song, hear me call-ing your name.
coun-try lane, I'll be sing-ing a song, hear me call-ing your name.

Hear the wind whis-per in the trees, tell-ing Moth-er Na-ture 'bout
Hear the wind whis-per in the trees, tell-ing Moth-er Na-ture 'bout

you and me.
you and me.

D. S. %️ al Coda

Coda

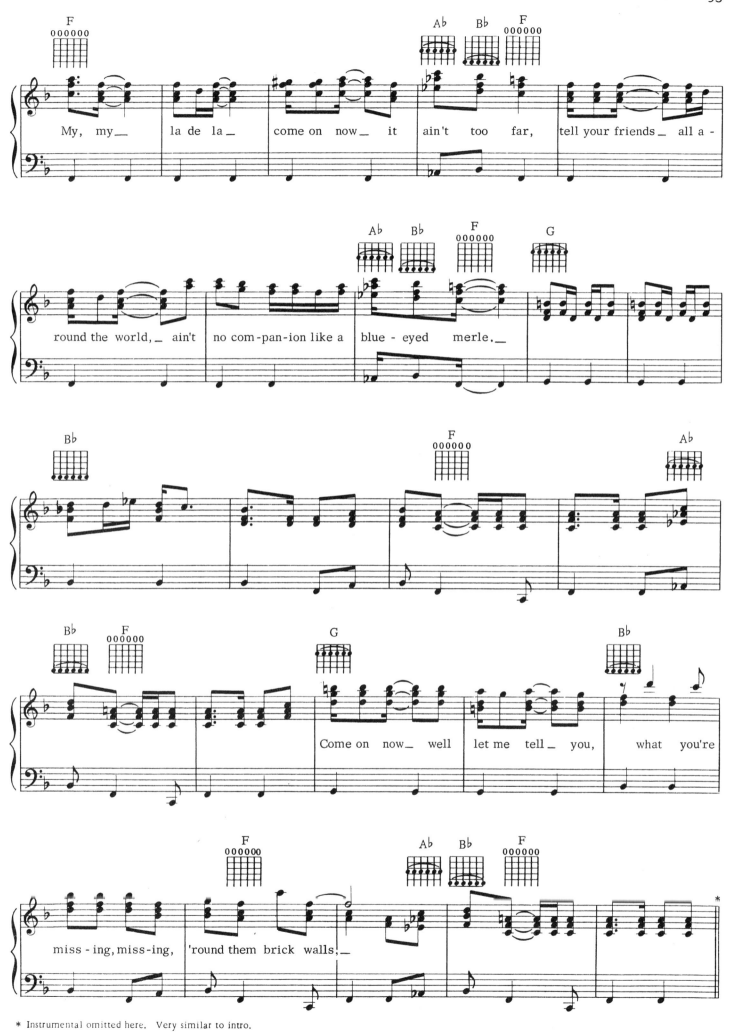

* Instrumental omitted here. Very similar to intro.

CELEBRATION DAY

Words and Music by
JIMMY PAGE, ROBERT PLANT
and JOHN PAUL JONES

voice is sore from shout-ing, cheer-ing win-ners who are los-ing, and she wor-ries if their days are few
walk you're gonna get there tho' it takes a lit-tle longer, and when you see it in the distance you will

1st time: *Skip these two bars*
2nd time: *Repeat and Fade*

Coda

and soon they'll have to
wring your hands and moan.

go.

My, my, my, I'm so hap-py, I'm gon-na join the band,___

name is Brown or White or Black, _ you know her ver-y well, _ you hear her cries of mer-cy as the

win-ners toll the bell.

My, my, my,

I'm so hap-py, I'm _ gon-na join the band, _____

FRIENDS

Words and Music by
JIMMY PAGE and ROBERT PLANT

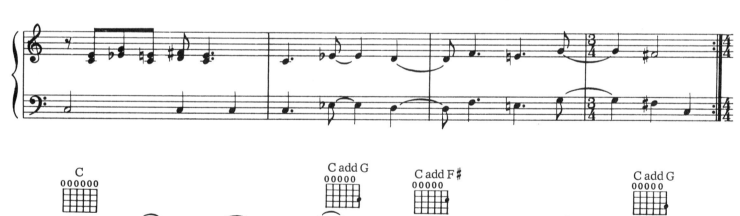

Bright light__ al - most blind - ing, black night still there shin - ing,

* Special note to Guitarists: Use C tuning: 1st string = E   2nd string = C   3rd string = G
4th string = C   5th string = G   6th string = C

* Last 4 bars of 38-bar Ad lib. Coda in C major.

HATS OFF TO (ROY) HARPER

Traditional Arrangement by
CHARLES OBSCURE

Jimmy Page plays bottleneck guitar on this piece.

Tune guitar as follows: 6th string = C   3rd string = G
5th string = G   2nd string = C
4th string = C   1st string = E

The chords are all played as full, 6 string barre chords:

C is either open or a barre at the 12th fret.
E♭ is a barre at the 3rd fret.
F is a barre at the 5th fret.
G is a barre at the 7th fret.

Listen mama,

Gave my baby a twenty dollar bill,

If that don't get her, sure my shot, shot, shot-gun will,

Yeah, I gave my baby a twenty dollar bill,

If that don't get that woman, I'm sure my shot-gun will.

LED ZEPPELIN IV

BLACK DOG

Words and Music by
JIMMY PAGE, ROBERT PLANT
and JOHN PAUL JONES

Medium beat

No chords

Hey, hey, ma - ma, said the way you move__ gon - na make you sweat,__ gon - na

make you groove.__

Oh, oh, child,__ way you shake that thing__ gon - na

make you burn,__ gon - na make you sting.__

Hey, hey, ba - by, when you walk that way __ watch your

hon - ey drip, __ can't keep a - way. __

dreams of you___ all thru my head.___

Ah ah ah ah ah ah ah ah

ah ah ah ah ah._____ Hey,

baby, oh, ba - by, pret - ty ba - by, la la la la

116

FOUR STICKS

Words and Music by
JIMMY PAGE and ROBERT PLANT

MISTY MOUNTAIN HOP

Words and Music by
JIMMY PAGE, ROBERT PLANT
and JOHN PAUL JONES

Moderate Rock

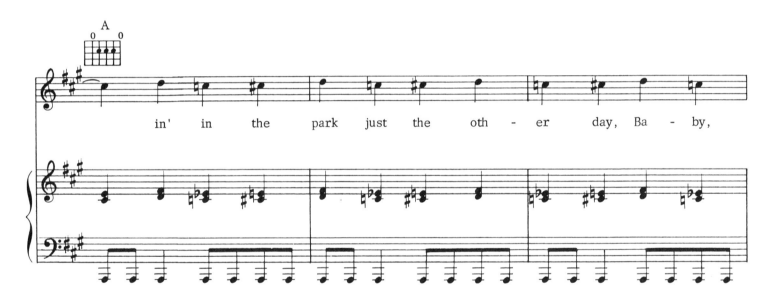

then a po-lice-man stepped up to me and asked us said, "Please, hey, would we care

to all get in line,____ get in line."

Well you know, they asked us to stay for tea_ and

have some fun,____ oh,_ oh,____ he said that his friends_

WHEN THE LEVEE BREAKS

Words and Music by
JIMMY PAGE, ROBERT PLANT,
JOHN PAUL JONES, JOHN BONHAM
and MEMPHIS MINNIE

Moderate Rock

last night ___ sat on the lev - ee and moaned, ___

think - in' 'bout my ba - by and ___ my hap - py home. ___

STAIRWAY TO HEAVEN

Words and Music by
JIMMY PAGE and ROBERT PLANT

There's a la - dy who's sure —— all that glit - ters is gold_ and she's buy - ing a stair - way —— to

142

roli.

And she's buy - ing a stair - way— to heav - en. —

ROCK AND ROLL

Words and Music by
JIMMY PAGE, ROBERT PLANT,
JOHN PAUL JONES and JOHN BONHAM

Moderately fast

Seems so long___ since we walked in the moon - light, mak - ing vows___ that just can't work___ right.___

O - pen your arms, o - pen your arms, o - pen your arms,___

GOING TO CALIFORNIA

Words and Music by
JIMMY PAGE and ROBERT PLANT

wake.

Seems that the wrath— of the Gods— got a punch— on the nose— and it start-ed to flow;—

— I think I might be sink - ing.

Throw me a line— if I reach— it in time— I'll meet—

THE BATTLE OF EVERMORE

Words and Music by
JIMMY PAGE and ROBERT PLANT

163

164

LED ZEPPELIN V

THE CRUNGE

Words and Music by
JOHN BONHAM, JOHN PAUL JONES,
JIMMY PAGE and ROBERT PLANT

175

176

180

D'YER MAK'ER

Words and Music by
JOHN BONHAM, JOHN PAUL JONES
and ROBERT PLANT

OVER THE HILLS AND FAR AWAY

Words and Music by
JIMMY PAGE and ROBERT PLANT

Man-y have_ I loved,_ and man-y times_ been bit-ten,

man-y times_I've gazed _____ a - long the o - pen road._

THE RAIN SONG

Words and Music by
JIMMY PAGE and ROBERT PLANT

glow - ing,   I watched the fire   that __ grew so   low, _____

202

DANCING DAYS

Words and Music by
JIMMY PAGE and ROBERT PLANT

Moderately, with a beat

Danc-ing days are here

Is that the way it should start? ___ I know it is - n't.

THE OCEAN

Words and Music by
JOHN BONHAM, JOHN PAUL JONES,
JIMMY PAGE and ROBERT PLANT

Got no__ time to pack__ my bag, __ my foot's out - side the door, __

I got a date, I can't __ be late for the high hopes hail-a ball. _____

Four times
N.C.

Four times

Sing - ing to an o - cean, I can hear the o - cean's roar, __

real fine way to start.

NO QUARTER

Words and Music by
JOHN PAUL JONES,
JIMMY PAGE and ROBERT PLANT

the winds of Thor _ are blow - ing cold.

A (addB)   A   A (addB)

They're wear-ing steel _ that's bright _ and true, _____

mf

D sus +4

they car-ry news _ that must _ get through. _

C#m
4 fr.

They choose the path _ where no _ one goes, ___

THE SONG REMAINS THE SAME

Words and Music by
JIMMY PAGE and ROBERT PLANT